AF399759

NEGOTIATING YOUR SALARY

Get the money and recognition you deserve

Written by Isabelle Aussant
Translated by Rebecca Neal

Coaching 50MINUTES.com

NEGOTIATING YOUR SALARY

- **Problem:** how can you bring up your salary when you receive a job offer or a promotion? What methods should you use to successfully negotiate your salary?
- **Uses:** negotiation is a vital skill during job interviews or promotions in order to make sure that your salary matches up with your expectations and skills.
- **Professional context:** human resources, annual performance review, new job, promotion, professional development, conflict resolution.
- **FAQs:**
  - What should I do if my employer refuses to give me a pay rise?
  - How should I formulate my request for a pay rise?
  - Is there an ideal time to negotiate?
  - What arguments should I use when negotiating?
  - Can I negotiate my salary during the recruit-

ment phase?
  ◦ What qualities do I need to become a good negotiator?

Talking about money is not easy, and we often do not dare to bring it up to managers or recruiters. According to a study published by Harvard Business School, almost half of recent American graduates do not negotiate their salary for their first job, mainly because they lack negotiating experience. It is true that salary negotiations can be delicate, and they require preparation. However, they are an inescapable part of professional life, and if we do not prepare effectively for them, great opportunities may end up passing us by.

During performance reviews, job interviews or promotions, negotiation should be a time for discussion rather than a source of conflict. You must be able to set out your arguments and clearly explain your needs and desires to the other person. In a way, these discussions are similar to a game, in that they are governed by rules and codes that you must master if you want to give yourself the best possible chance of reaching a satisfactory agreement.

EFFECTIVE NEGOTIATION: THE BASICS

The word "negotiate" comes from the Latin *negōtiārī*, meaning "to do business". It therefore refers to a discussion between two parties who are looking for an agreement that satisfies everyone's expectations. During this exchange, each person states their needs and sets out their arguments to try and convince the other side. It is therefore essential to prepare for this discussion, in order to anticipate how it will play out, the questions that will be asked and any potential stumbling blocks. This will increase your chances of getting what you want out of the meeting.

PREPARING TO NEGOTIATE

Julien Bertheau works as a property manager, has had five different employers in the past ten years and has had to negotiate his salary eight times. He says:

<blockquote>"To negotiate successfully, you need to define your objectives, know your value and the market by researching similar posts, and make sure that your work justifies your request."[1]</blockquote>

Assess your career so far

The first step before a job interview is to draw up a factual evaluation of your strong points, weak points and areas for improvement. Specifically, you have to know both your personal and professional assets and weaknesses.

Start by going over your career so far and the different posts you have held, making a note of the skills you demonstrated and acquired for each of them. You also need to think about the difficulties you faced, as this will enable you to identify your strong points and areas for improvement.

<blockquote>"I was a Key Account Manager at a company from 2008 to 2012. In the course of my work, the customers I dealt with were mainly Spanish-speaking, which allowed me to improve my</blockquote>

---

1. This quotation has been translated by 50Minutes.com.

Spanish. After four years in the position, I learnt to speak and write it fluently without too much difficulty." (Paul, account manager)

Drawing up this assessment will make you aware of your professional value and allow you to answer the following questions: what can I bring to a company or a team that other people cannot? What added value do I bring? Highlight your knowledge of foreign languages, your specific areas of expertise, your professional contacts, your temperament, and so on, using concrete facts to back up your points. This will allow you to identify your assets to support your salary negotiation, but also your limitations so that you can anticipate any questions or comments that the other person may have about them.

If you want to secure a pay rise, make a note of the projects you have worked on throughout the year. Collect these examples and use them when you are negotiating to support your request and prove how much you have contributed to the company.

Know the market

Research how much your post is worth: what salaries are typical for the same job, with the same levels of skill, experience and responsibility? If you are interviewing for a new job, gather information about your future job in advance: what tasks will the position involve? What will the pace of work be like? What responsibilities will you have? This will allow you to justify the amount you are asking for by using concrete facts.

Having an objective estimation of your "market value" is an essential first step in any negotiation, as it shows that you understand the market and boosts your credibility. Your value can vary depending on your circumstances: for example, your value is higher if a recruiter has contacted you than if you are responding to an advert. The fact that a recruiter has reached out to you means that they are interested in your profile, which puts you in a stronger position to secure a salary that matches up to your expectations. If a recruiter wants to poach you from your current company, they will have to make you an attractive offer to compensate for the risks you are running: loss of seniority, trial period, moving, and so on. On the other hand, if you are just one candidate among many others, your arguments will need to be more convincing.

Research the company's financial situation

If you are applying for a job, research the company you are applying to. This will allow you to get to know it better and evaluate what it can offer you. Research the company's turnover, its growth, future prospects in the sector, any recent reorganisations, internal salary practices, the salaries offered by its major competitors, and so on. Does the company offer individual or collective pay rises? If so, does it offer them regularly? Annual reports for many companies can be found online or in specialised publications. Being informed during your interview will show that you are committed and motivated, which could tip the scales in your favour.

If you are being promoted or asking for a pay rise, research your company's profits for the last year.

Define your needs and expectations

In order to establish an appropriate salary bracket, start by evaluating your needs: rent, dependants, taxes, and so on. This will allow you to define your BATNA and your ZOPA.

- Your **BATNA** (Best Alternative to a Negotiated Agreement) is the most advantageous solution for you.
- Your **ZOPA** (Zone of Possible Agreement) fol-

lows on logically from your BATNA and is used to determine the concessions that both sides are prepared to accept.

Defining what you expect in terms of salary is an essential step so that you are prepared when the other person brings up numbers. Take the time to think carefully: your salary will have a direct impact on your professional and personal life and on your wellbeing.

Money is not everything

The best offer does not always mean the highest salary! You should think about your career as a whole when negotiating your salary, which means that you will need to shift your perception of your future salary slightly to look at your professional development more broadly. For example, some professional opportunities will allow you to progress more quickly than others or to acquire expertise that will later give you a competitive advantage on the market. As a result, you need to think about the future. Ask yourself the following questions:

- What can this post do for me?

- What skills will I use and develop?
- How well-known is the company that wants to recruit me?
- What impact will the post have on my career?

Anticipate possible objections

If the other person puts forward an objection, that does not necessarily mean that they are not open to discussion. In most cases, they are trying to test you and give you the chance to prove yourself with your answer. This is therefore the ideal moment to win them over.

Before any negotiation, list any criticisms (whether they are legitimate or not) that could be levelled at your arguments, then sort them into two categories:

- **Closed objections**, for which you will already have prepared an answer.

- **Open or tactical objections**, which may be unfounded and are raised with the aim of throwing you off balance. You should anticipate and be ready to respond to comments along the lines of "I need to think about it", "I understand where you're coming from, but times are hard", and "You don't have the skills or the potential". Find answers to turn the situation in your favour.

- find and suggest solutions that are acceptable to both parties;
- continue with the discussion and make sure that the objection has been fully resolved by checking that the other person agrees with you ("Do you agree?", "Does that work for you?").

Manage your stress

Stress is more or less inevitable in this kind of situation. Mental preparation is therefore essential to avoid letting stress get the better of you, which could hamper your negotiation and leave you feeling angry with yourself later. Remember that stress results from fixating on worst-case scenarios, and that the doubts that arise from imagining the worst serve no purpose and wear you out mentally.

Facing up to your fears when you prepare will take away their power and boost your determination. Be confident: if you are well prepared, you have every chance of success. Take some deep breaths a few minutes before the interview to calm your nerves, then go for it.

Reasoned negotiation

There are different types of negotiation. If you want to obtain a result that is satisfactory for both parties, opt for reasoned negotiation or win-win negotiation. This approach, developed by Roger Fisher (1922-2012) and William Ury (born in 1953), negotiation experts and founders of the Harvard Negotiation Project, does not aim to fully satisfy the needs of each party, as this would be impossible, but rather to reach a fair agreement after a reasoned discussion. The two researchers contrast this method with distributive negotiation, in which both sides try to maximise their gains without taking the other's needs into account. This results in a win-lose situation, or even a lose-lose situation if the negotiation fails.

Reasoned negotiation	Distributive negotiation
Both parties win.	One party wins and the other loses (in a worst-case scenario, both parties lose).
Considering each side's needs and underlying interests.	Each side sticks to their guns until one side gives in or the negotiation fails.
Finding a compromise by making concessions.	Being willing to resort to any means necessary to have your demands met.
Treating people and objectives separately.	Using threats or pressure.

This win-win relationship is the ideal solution and allows you to negotiate your salary in an atmosphere of trust and respect. You will leave the meeting feeling satisfied and recognised, and the other person will feel that the salary you have negotiated is fair.

The right attitudes

Effective communication is crucial if you want your interview to go well. There are two main channels for communication, which you need to keep in mind, as they will be a valuable help during negotiation:

- **Verbal language**. If you have prepared well, you will have carefully selected and organised your arguments. Watch out for verbal tics, fillers and meaningless expressions like "do you see what I mean?", "right?" and "well". Listening is indispensable in communication: observe the other person, look them in the eye and analyse what they are saying. Do not hesitate to ask them for extra information or to reword what they have said to make sure that you have fully understood: taking an interest in what the other person is saying will make them feel valued. Use wording like "if I've understood correctly" and "so the important points are...". Although verbal language is obviously important, it only makes up a small percentage of our communication, with most of the impact coming from body language.
- **Body language**. Our behaviour, posture, gestures, way of speaking and tone of voice are all important, because we transmit indirect messages through our bodies. Paul Watzlawick (Austrian-born psychologist and sociologist, 1921-2007) claims that we communicate all the time, even when we are not speaking, because our body conveys information about our state

of mind. The following tips will help you to project a positive image:

Your posture	**Tips:** • Standing or sitting up straight will give an impression of confidence and assurance. • Leaning slightly towards the other person shows that you are interested in them. **Things to avoid:** • If you are too relaxed or turned to one side when sitting down, this may be interpreted as presumptuousness or a lack of interest. • Perching on the edge of your seat or sitting with your ankles wrapped around the chair legs suggests anxiety or a lack of self-confidence.
Your gestures	**Tip:** • Large, sweeping gestures indicate assurance and a willingness to engage. **Things to avoid:** • Crossing your hands or tapping your fingers on the table will make you seem tense and withdrawn.

Your expressions	**Tip:** • Looking directly at the other person with a broad, spontaneous smile indicates your interest and open-mindedness. **Things to avoid:** • Frowning or pursing your lips suggests inner tension. • Failing to meet the other person's eye indicates embarrassment or a lack of self-confidence. • Letting your mouth hang open or raising your eyebrows may suggest a degree of scepticism.
Your voice	**Tips:** • Pay attention to the volume of your voice; do not speak too loudly or too quietly. • Express yourself clearly and comprehensibly. **Things to avoid:** • Mumbling and speaking too slowly. • Talking too quickly indicates nerves. • Speaking too loudly could be interpreted as a sign of arrogance or presumptuousness.

Adapt your approach to the other person

You can increase your chances of success by adapting your behaviour to the manager or recruiter's personality. If you get the opportunity before the interview, think about them, analyse them and work out what they are like. Try to figure out what matters to them: time spent at the office, results, cultural fit, and so on. This will allow you to adjust what you say and adopt the same language as them. We can identify four personality types:

- **Experts** are rational and logical, and value facts and precision. Opt for a well-structured, technical argument with concrete figures and achievements: mention the budgets you handled, quantitative objectives and reports.
- **Organisers** are meticulous and relatively resistant to change. They value routine and emphasise practical details and methods. Take a thorough, reassuring approach and provide detailed examples ("As part of this project, I used this tool or that method").
- **Communicators** are extroverted, open and talkative. They value human contact and spontaneous exchanges. Establish a warm, friendly relationship with them by talking about your experiences ("During this project, I met so-and-so, and I learned a lot from their decision-making ability. Now we are very close professionally").
- **Strategists** are creative, visionary and intuitive, and value overall visions and innovative perspectives. Provide original illustrations for your argument and highlight projects where you demonstrated creativity.

FORMULATING YOUR REQUEST

It is finally time to negotiate. Whether you are being interviewed for a job or asking for a pay raise, you are now ready and there is nothing standing in the way of you getting what you want.

The right moment

Choose the right moment. Some times are better than others for negotiating your salary, as outlined in the table below.

Good times	<ul><li>After a positive performance review: companies generally organise an annual review for each employee, so take this opportunity to bring up your salary.</li><li>After at least six months to a year into your job.</li><li>After a successful project: your achievements will make for good arguments.</li><li>When things are going well for the company: a business that is making big profits will more readily pass them on to its employees.</li><li>When you change role or status: it is natural for your salary to increase if you take on new responsibilities.</li><li>At the end of your trial period: if your employer mentioned it during the interview, do not be afraid to bring the subject up again. Some contracts specify a salary increase at the end of the trial period.</li></ul>
Times to avoid	<ul><li>Crisis periods (restructuring, budget calculations, and so on): if things are not going well at your company, your employer will not be inclined to increase your salary.</li><li>After salaries have already been adjusted. If they are adjusted in January, there is no point trying to negotiate in March.</li><li>When you have just come back from holiday. Get stuck back into your work first to prove your motivation to your boss.</li></ul>

If you are interviewing for a job, bring the subject up at the end of the interview. In general, the recruiter will mention it themselves, but if they do not, do not hesitate to ask the question. If you are already working for the company, wait until your annual performance review to discuss a potential pay rise with your manager. If you are promoted or change roles, talk about the salary when you are told about your new position.

Salary negotiation techniques

As we have already discussed, before any negotiation you should set a salary objective based on both your needs and the realities of the market. But what should you do during the interview itself? Should you open with a higher figure? How should you react if the figure you are given is far lower than the one you imagined?

The career management specialist Daniel Porot advises using the eight second technique to increase the offer: once the other person has told you the amount they are proposing, repeat it in a neutral tone, then stay silent for eight seconds. Keep looking them in the eyes and do not show any emotion. In doing so, you will make them doubt themselves, which will push them to offer a higher figure. Porot adds that, if the recruiter is going to change their mind, they will do it on the fourth or fifth second rather than the eighth. If this does not work, Porot suggest seven other negotiation strategies:

Salary negotiation strategies

The cake	Represent the company's profits in the form of a cake, then calculate the impact of your work on it and ask for your share.
The springboard	Agree to start off with a lower salary on the condition that it is accompanied by a written promise of a raise after a few months.
Part-time	Offer to work part-time if that situation works for you and the company's budget genuinely cannot cover the salary you want.
Competition	Tell the other person that you have other offers and mention the highest salary offered by one of their competitors.

The welcome bonus	If you are already working and somebody tries to poach you, negotiate a welcome bonus for joining them.
The bracket	Put forward a salary bracket between the salary of the employees you manage and that of your direct superior.
The study	Cite figures from a study featuring salaries for your position. Basing your argument on a real study will give you greater credibility.

USING YOUR MONTHLY SALARY TO NEGOTIATE

If the annual salary the other person gives you is much lower than you expected, frame the subsequent discussion in terms of your monthly salary instead: the difference between the two amounts will be much lower and it will be easier to reach a mutually satisfying compromise.

Mistakes to avoid

To reach your objectives, avoid falling into the following traps:

- Asking for less to be sure that you will get the job (if you are applying for a new job). You risk ending up feeling undervalued when you are working there and thinking "I could have got more".
- Asking for too much, as this may make you look greedy. Keep your expectations realistic.
- Justifying your pay increase by saying that you need the money. Your employer will give you a salary or a pay rise based on the work you do for them, not on your personal needs.
- Comparing your salary to a colleague's, or putting them down to justify your value. This will reflect badly on you.
- Threatening to work less. You will be viewed as someone who is untrustworthy and does not honour their commitments.
- Pretending to stop negotiating. What will you do if this strategy fails?
- Trying to get what you want by flirting or any other inappropriate, unprofessional behaviour.
- Putting the difficult questions off until later.

- Bargaining ("I'll give you that if you'll give me this").
- Appealing to the other person's emotions (friendship, respect, habit of working together, and so on).
- Telling a recruiter that you are quitting your current job so you can earn more. They will think that you are more interested in the salary than the role, and will move on to a more motivated candidate.

the same page as you and feel comfortable in the conversation.
- You are persuasive. Are you using the right words? Are you backing up what you say with proof?

Conclude the negotiation

It is now time to conclude your interview and reach an initial oral agreement. If your request is justified by your arguments, you have established a positive relationship with the other person and they have not made any sincere objections, you have a strong chance of achieving your objective. The following signs typically indicate that a conclusion is near:

- the other person asks you an additional question about your profile or asks you if you would be prepared to take on another task as well as your official role;
- the other person half-heartedly revisits an objection;
- the other person makes a false objection;
- the other person asks you basic questions;
- the other person makes sure that they have

TOP TIPS

- **Read between the lines:** employers never ask questions for no reason. An apparently trivial question may be their way of trying to obtain a piece of information that they consider crucial. For example, if a recruiter asks you whether you have applied for any other positions, they are almost certainly trying to find out how urgently they need to act if they want to hire you and how in demand you are on the job market.
- **Be "hireable":** this means letting the other person think that another employer is very interested in you, while at the same time implying that they have a strong chance of hiring you. Be careful here! You need to find the right balance: dropping this kind of hint should speed up the process, but if you do not play your cards right you may discourage the employer from competing for you.
- **Do not take things the wrong way:** the other person may try to strengthen their hand by saying things that sound like ultimatums. Do not pay attention to them: they are just

conscious or subconscious techniques to rush you or intimidate you. Take note of them by saying "I hear what you're saying" in a neutral tone, but do not react immediately to the proposition.

- **Avoid bringing up your old salary:** if your previous salary was significantly lower than the amount you are hoping for now, do not mention it. However, do not lie if you are asked about it directly. This risks damaging the recruiter's view of you, as nowadays it is easy for them to find this information out for themselves. An effective way of dealing with the question is to explain that your old salary was set based on older criteria or that you had different responsibilities.
- **Make suggestions:** get the other person's attention by making suggestions that could help them and make their life easier. These could include an idea for a project, new responsibilities, a new organisational system, and so on. If you are an asset for them and for the company, they will be more likely to give you the salary you are asking for.
- **Pay attention:** in his book *Méthodes et astuces pour... mieux négocier* ("Methods and Tips to

Negotiate Better"), the negotiation consultant Richard Bourrelly claims that good negotiators listen twice as much as they speak. Take what the other person is saying on board and show them that you are interested.

- **Know your place:** remember that the person you are talking to is your (future) boss. Steer the negotiation, but leave the final decision up to them. Do not try to lead the debate, as this may cause them to dig their heels in and put an end to the discussion.
- **Be precise:** employees who put forward precise proposals are typically seen as being better informed about the market. If you adopt this approach, the other person will think that they have less room for manoeuvre and accept your request more readily.
- **Be prepared to accept a lower salary:** if the salary you are offered is lower than the amount you were hoping for, you can accept it while asking for an increase at a later date based on the fulfilment of certain objectives.
- **Do not be the first to bring the subject up:** as a general rule, the recruiter should be the first one to talk about salary. However, if they do not mention it, go for it: it is a reasonable

question, so you should not feel uncomfortable or embarrassed. That said, make sure that you wait until the end of the interview, as the first part is supposed to be a chance for you to present your experience and skills in order to back up your request.

Stay positive

Take a positive view of your negotiation. Use the technique of autosuggestion: have confidence in yourself so that others will have confidence in you. You will only convince the other person if you believe in what you are saying. Keep telling yourself that you will be successful, as this will allow you to go into the interview feeling more confident.

FAQS

WHAT SHOULD I DO IF MY EMPLOYER REFUSES TO GIVE ME A PAY RISE?

Try to understand why they are against your arguments and find alternative solutions. Above all, do not give up at the first sign of a setback! Negotiating requires patience and a lot of perseverance. Listen to their arguments and state your own. Discussing the matter should enable you to reach a compromise.

HOW SHOULD I FORMULATE MY REQUEST FOR A PAY RISE?

You can either use a precise amount or request a particular percentage. Do the maths and clearly define your objective before giving the employer your figure. Asking for an increase by a net amount per month may seem less sizeable to them and get lost in the rest of the salary budget, especially if the company has a lot of employees. That said, do not get too hung up on numbers and work out what you will actually end up taking home. For example, if your current gross salary is £35 000 per year and you ask for an increase of 10% (meaning roughly £290 gross or £200 net per month), this percentage may seem high. However, if you say that you want a monthly pay rise of £300 gross, this will seem less significant and you will be more likely to get what you want. How you present your request matters!

IS THERE AN IDEAL TIME TO NEGOTIATE?

If only there were! Unfortunately, this is a myth and can become an excuse to avoid taking the plunge. Having said that, some periods are better than others. You can give yourself the best possible chance of success by negotiating in the following situations:

- just after your annual performance review (only if it was positive, of course);
- after a professional success in the company;
- if the company is doing well;
- if you are moving into a new role with new

responsibilities;

- at the end of your trial period;
- during the recruitment phase, at the end of the interview once you have proved that you are person for the job.

You should also avoid Mondays, as people often have a lot of work and emails to deal with, and Fridays, because your employer may already be thinking about the weekend. Instead, opt for a Tuesday or a Thursday. Finally, early in the day is better, as the other person is less likely to be hungry and irritable; alternatively, negotiate in the middle of the afternoon rather than at the end of the day.

WHAT ARGUMENTS SHOULD I USE WHEN NEGOTIATING?

Your request will only be justified if it is based on solid arguments. Give concrete, convincing reasons to prove that your presence has benefitted or will benefit the company. Do not hesitate to mention the objectives that you have already achieved. Highlight points that will be particularly impressive to the other person by employing the criteria that they use to evaluate productivity and the different kinds of accomplishments that matter most to them.

CAN I NEGOTIATE MY SALARY DURING THE RECRUITMENT PHASE?

Absolutely! But keep in mind that the recruiter should be the first to bring up the subject. If you are too quick to mention it, they may think that you are more interested in the salary than in the role and the responsibilities that come with it. More importantly, you may end up telling them a lower amount than you could have ended up with! Let them talk first: the amount they suggest may well surprise you.

NEGOTIATING DURING THE RECRUITMENT PHASE

During the recruitment process, never talk about salary before receiving a firm job offer. Put yourself in a position of strength rather than vulnerability. Base your request on concrete facts and do not rush into things!

WHAT QUALITIES DO I NEED TO BECOME A GOOD NEGOTIATOR?

To become an effective negotiator:

- Pay attention to the other person, react to what they are saying and prove that you are interested.
- Keep your cool when you and your employer disagree. Getting angry will only make things worse.
- Be determined, but remember that your final objective is to reach a compromise. If a disagreement arises, do not give up and try to find solutions to overcome it.
- Stand your ground. Believe in yourself and do not give in to unjustified objections. However, be prepared to back down a little if the other person proposes a reasonable compromise.
- Be imaginative. If the discussion is going round in circles, offer new solutions that could satisfy both sides.
- Make the most of your strengths. This does not mean charming the other person, but rather impressing them with your professionalism. You can do this by speaking clearly, respecting

your employer, dressing well and putting forward strong arguments about your value to the company.

OVER TO YOU

LIST YOUR QUALITIES

To begin with, select three of your qualities, then describe a professional situation where you demonstrated each of them. Finally, identify the assets that will allow to reach your aims in the negotiation and base your strategy on them.

Your qualities	Professional situations
Quality 1:	
Quality 2:	
Quality 3:	

BELIEVE IN YOURSELF SO THAT OTHERS WILL BELIEVE IN YOU

As we have already seen, every time you negotiate you need to prepare in advance. In order to formulate convincing arguments, list your greatest personal and professional successes, such as:

- Success in an exam. Remember the moment when you saw your mark.
- Landing an important market. How did you manage it?
- Winning a sporting competition. Remember the moment when the match turned in your favour.
- A promotion at work. How did you feel?

Reliving these experiences will make you feel successful, increase your self-confidence and provide concrete, convincing examples for the other person.

NEGOTIATION PRACTICE

Practice debating with a friend. Set out your arguments and objections over a set time and work on how you formulate your points, the tone of your voice, the relevance of your arguments, and any other details that will help you on the big day. Once you have finished the negotiation, analyse the strong and weak points in your arguments.

Feel free to switch roles: putting yourself in your employer's shoes will give you a different point of view. You can also ask your friend to adopt different personalities and pretend to be a narrow-minded, arrogant or aggressive employer. This will give you the practice you need to react effectively in any situation.

FURTHER READING

BIBLIOGRAPHY

- Bourrelly, R. (2007) *Méthodes et astuces pour... mieux négocier.* Paris: Éditions Eyrolles.

- Giang, V. (2013) 7 Negotiation Tips Given To Harvard Business School Students. *Business Insider.* [Online]. [Accessed 2 October 2017]. Available from: <http://www.businessinsider.com/harvard-professor-gives-tips-on-negotiating-2013-8?IR=T>

- Harlé, I. and Traverson, M. (2007) *Réussissez toute vos négos en entreprise.* Paris: Éditions L'Express.

- Porot, D. and Bolles Haynes, F. (2001) *101 Ways to Improve Your Salary.* Berkeley, California: Ten Speed Press.

50MINUTES.com
History
Business
Coaching
Book Review
Health & Wellbeing
ISHIKAWA DIAGRAM
Anticipate and solve problems within your business
Material Method Machine
Mother Nature Measure Men
Business 50MINUTES.com
THE BATTLE OF AUSTERLITZ
NETWORKING